I Hope This Brings You Both Much Pleasure!
Enjoy!

This Coupon Entitles You To:

Some TV Ad Break Fun
(For One Movie Or TV Show She Must Pleasure
You When The Adverts Come On & Stop
When They Finish Each Time)

This Coupon Entitles You To:

One No Hands Session
(Both Get Naked, Then You Are Both
Forbidden To Use Your Hands On Each Other
Anything Else Goes)

This Coupon Entitles You To:

Blindfold Her
(She Must Lick, Suck, Nibble Anything
That Is Put In Front Of Her)

This Coupon Entitles You To:

Cum Where Ever You
Choose

This Coupon Entitles You To:

Tie Her Up And Do What
You Want With Her

This Coupon Entitles You To:

One Super Sloppy Blowjob
(The Wetter, The Better)

This Coupon Entitles You To:

Watch Porn Together

This Coupon Entitles You To:

Receive An Oil Massage
Where You Are Both
Naked

This Coupon Entitles You To:

One Spontaneous Blowjob,
(She Must Suck Your Dick
When You Are Not Expecting It)

This Coupon Entitles You To:

Watch Her Clean The
House While She Is
Topless

This Coupon Entitles You To:

Pick And Use Any Sex Toy
On Her

This Coupon Entitles You To:

Buy A Suction Dildo And
Have A Three Some With It
(Stick The Dildo To The Tiles And She Can
Fuck It While She Sucks You Dry)

This Coupon Entitles You To:

A Skirt & No Panties
Night Out
(You Can Choose Where You Go, And She
Must Go Commando)

This Coupon Entitles You To:

Public Sex
(Find Somewhere Quiet, Don't Get Caught)

This Coupon Entitles You To:

Play With Her Ass

(She Must Let You Either Rub, Lick, Finger
Or Fuck It, Or All If She Agrees)

This Coupon Entitles You To:

Receive One Blowjob While
Watching Sports Or Your
Favourite Show

This Coupon Entitles You To:

Be The Director And Take
Dirty Pics Of Her
(She Must Follow Your Every Instruction
From Which Positions, Outfit And Action)

This Coupon Entitles You To:

One Shower Sex Session
(Start By Washing Each Other's Bodies)

This Coupon Entitles You To:

Receive Naughty Pictures
From Your Partner
(For One Day While You Are
Out Of The House)

This Coupon Entitles You To:

One No Bra Day

(Your Partner Must Not Wear A Bra For The
Whole Day And Wear A Tight Or Low Cut Top
)

This Coupon Entitles You To:

A Teasing Thigh Massage
(Wearing No Underwear, She Must Give You
A Thigh Massage While Teasing You By
Getting Very Close To Your Manhood)

This Coupon Entitles You To:

Choose A Sexy Outfit For
Her To Wear
(Schoolgirl? Nurse? Secretary? It's Your
Choice)

This Coupon Entitles You To:

A Night Of Roleplay

(Choose The Scenario Eg; Strangers At A
Club, You're A Handyman Coming To Fix
Something, Taxi Driver, Etc And Make It
Happen)

This Coupon Entitles You To:

One Dirty Talk Session

(She Must Be Vocal And Tell You What She
Wants You To Do To Her And Want She
Wants To Do To You)

This Coupon Entitles You To:

One Just The Tip Blowjob
(She Can Only Lick And Suck The Head Of
Your Cock Until You Tell Her To Go Deeper)

This Coupon Entitles You To:

A Rough Sex Session

(Agree On A Safe Word And Both Be More
Forceful With Each Other, Think Choking,
Slapping, Pushing, Biting)

This Coupon Entitles You To:

One Day Of Flashing

(While At Home, She Must Flash You When
Ever You Request For Eg; Show Me Your
Tits, Show Me Your Ass, Etc)

This Coupon Entitles You To:

One Superior Handjob

(She Must Give You A Sexy Handjob And
Use Her Other Hand To Pleasure Herself
While You Watch)

This Coupon Entitles You To:

One Mirror Sex Session
(Find The Best Mirror In House & Have Sex,
Oral In Front Of It While You Both Watch)

This Coupon Entitles You To:

One Super Sloppy Blowjob
(The Wetter, The Better)

This Coupon Entitles You To:

One Bondage Session
(She Ties You Up And Blindfolds You And
You Must Do As She Tells You)

This Coupon Entitles You To:

One Teasing Car Session

(When You Are In The Car Together, She
Must Rub, Play With Your Cock Every Time
You Stop At Traffic Lights)

This Coupon Entitles You To:

One Sweet Sex Session
(Choose Some Items Eg; Chocolate Sauce, Honey, Strawberries, Whipped Cream And Eat, Lick Them Off Each Other's Bodies)

This Coupon Entitles You To:

One Anywhere Goes
Sex Session
(You Choose Any Place In The House To
Have Sex Excluding Bedrooms. Stairs?
Kitchen Counter? Sofa?)

This Coupon Entitles You To:

Receive An Oral Performance

(She Must Perform Oral Sex On Whatever You
Choose For 5 - 10 Mins For Eg; Your Finger,
Banana, Cucumber, Ice Lolly)

This Coupon Entitles You To:

One Enhanced Bath
(She Must Run You A Bath, After 10 Minutes
She Must Come Back And Make You Cum)

This Coupon Entitles You To:

One Sexy Tit Wank

(She Must Use Her Breasts To
Pleasure You, And Make You
Cum All Over Them)

This Coupon Entitles You To:

One Creamy Facial
(She Must Be On Her Knees And She Will
Make You Cum All Over Her Face)

This Coupon Entitles You To:

One Welcome Home Surprise

(Within The Next Week When You Return Home
She Must Greet You On The Stairs, Couch, Bed
With With No Underwear And Her Legs Spread)

This Coupon Entitles You To:

Listen To An Erotic Audio
Book Together

This Coupon Entitles You To:

One Solo Session

(You Will Both Pleasure Yourselves Next To Each
Other Until You Cum, You Are Not Allowed
To Touch Each Other)

This Coupon Entitles You To:

This Coupon Entitles You To:

This Coupon Entitles You To:

This Coupon Entitles You To:

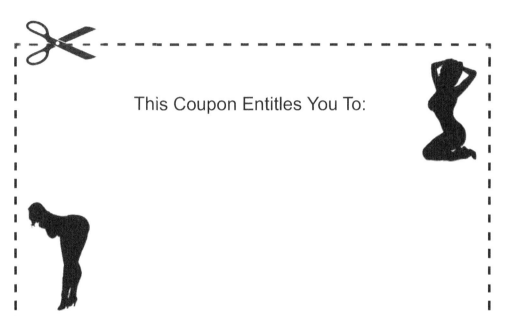

This Coupon Entitles You To:

This Coupon Entitles You To:

This Coupon Entitles You To:

This Coupon Entitles You To:

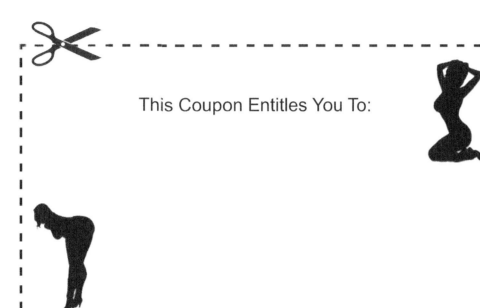

This Coupon Entitles You To:

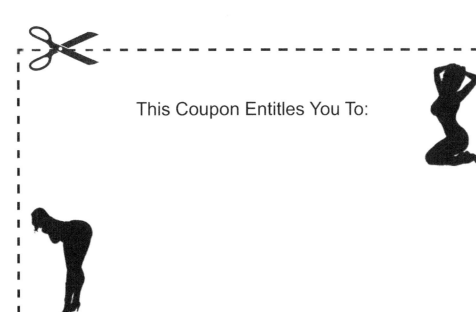

This Coupon Entitles You To:

Printed in Great Britain
by Amazon

29026542R00057